Artists Through the Ages

Edgar Degas

Alix Wood

WINDMILL BOOKS

New York

Published in 2015 by **Windmill Books,** An Imprint of Rosen Publishing
29 East 21st Street, New York, NY 10010

Editor for Alix Wood Books: Eloise Macgregor
Designer: Alix Wood

Photo Credits: Cover, 1, 7, 21 bottom, 23, 26, 27 © nga/Mr. and Mrs. Paul Mellon;
3, 5, 16 © Shutterstock; 4 © nga/Rosenwald Collection; 21 top © nga/Widener Collection;
29 © eff gynane/Shutterstock; 8 left © Sterlingand Francine Art Institute; 8 right © Yair
Haklai; 9, 17, 25 © Musée d'Orsay; 10© Cleveland Museum of Art; 11 © Walters Art
Museum; 12-13 © Musée des Beaux-Arts, Pau; 14 © Barber Institute of Fine Arts; 15 ©
National Gallery, London; 18 © Städel, Frankfurt; 19 © Hermitage Museum, St Petersburg;
22 © public domain; 28 © Minneapolis Society of Fine Arts; 29 © Harvard Art Museum/
Fogg Mueum

Library of Congress Cataloging-in-Publication Data

Wood, Alix.
 Edgar Degas / Alix Wood.
    pages cm. — (Artists through the ages)
 Includes index.
 ISBN 978-1-4777-5410-8 (pbk.)
 ISBN 978-1-4777-5411-5 (6 pack)
 ISBN 978-1-4777-5409-2 (library binding)
 1. Degas, Edgar, 1834-1917—Juvenile literature. 2. Artists—France—Biography—Juvenile
literature. I. Title.
 N6853.D33W655 2015
 709.2—dc23
 [B]
                            2014028205

Manufactured in the United States of America
CPSIA Compliance Information: Batch #CW15WM: For Further Information contact Windmill Books, New York, New York at 1-866-478-0556

Contents

Who Was Degas?

Edgar Degas was a French artist. He was best known for his paintings of dancers and horses. He was born in Paris, France in 1834. His real name was Hilaire-Germain-Edgar De Gas! He was the eldest of five children.

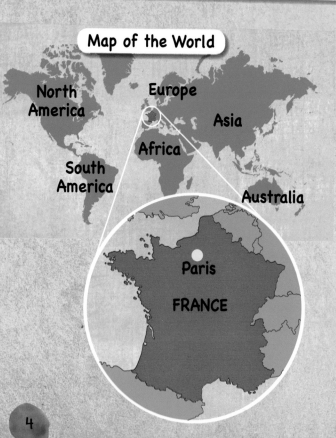

Map of the World

North America

Europe

Asia

Africa

South America

Australia

Paris

FRANCE

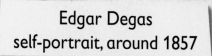

Edgar Degas
self-portrait, around 1857

Degas's mother was an opera singer and his father was a banker. Degas's mother died when he was 13 years old.

Copying the Masters

Degas was very good at art as a child. His father was an art lover and encouraged his talent. When he was 18 years old Degas got permission to "copy" at the famous Louvre art gallery in Paris. Young artists learned how to paint by copying the great paintings there.

Artists copying paintings in the Louvre, 1844

The Louvre gallery as it is today

Portrait Painter

Degas's father wanted him to go to law school. Degas started studying law at the University of Paris but he wasn't interested in the subject. Degas went instead to the best art school in Paris. He studied hard and turned a room in his home into an artist's **studio**. He met the painter Jean-Auguste-Dominique Ingres. Ingres encouraged Degas to keep drawing.

Some of Degas's first paintings were **portraits** of his family. The portrait opposite is of his brother, Achille. Degas loved to study people. Once, when fellow artist Walter Sickert suggested they take a cab to a café, Degas refused. He wanted to take the bus, so that he could look at people!

Bad Sitters

Degas's family were not well-behaved portrait subjects. They insisted that he paint their portraits in a style that they liked. Degas complained that they never kept still and they would sit in poor light.

Achille De Gas in the Uniform of a Cadet, around 1856

Visiting Family in Italy

After a year at art school, Degas traveled to Italy. He spent a lot of time in Rome studying the paintings of the great Italian painters.

Degas copied the works of famous Italian artists such as Michelangelo, Raphael, and Titian. Usually, students would copy a whole painting. Degas didn't. He would choose a little **detail** from the painting or sculpture instead.

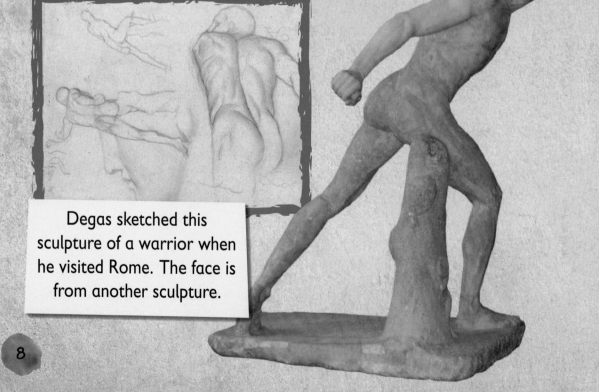

Degas sketched this sculpture of a warrior when he visited Rome. The face is from another sculpture.

The Bellilli Family

A Family Portrait

Degas stayed with his aunt, Laura Bellilli, in Naples, Italy. Degas's first great **masterpiece** was this painting of the Bellilli family. Degas sketched the family while he stayed with them. The family were not very happy at the time. Laura's brother, Degas's grandfather, had recently died. Can you see the dog walking out of the painting?

Painting Racehorses

Degas loved to paint racehorses. He created around 45 oil paintings, 20 **pastel** drawings, 250 pencil drawings, and 17 sculptures of horses. Degas was even said to have a full-size stuffed horse in his studio!

Drawing With Pastels

Degas used pastel crayons to create some of his work. Oil paint takes a long time to dry, so pastels were a quicker way to use color. Degas liked painting tense moments such as these horses and jockeys waiting for the race to start.

Race Horses, around 1873. Degas hardly ever painted the actual race, and never painted the exciting finish!

Before the Race, painted around 1883

Degas sometimes made wax models of racehorses
from his **sketches**. He could then arrange and
paint the model horses from different angles.
He often used the same horses and jockeys in
several paintings. He would make them bigger or
smaller, or flip them to face the other way, so that
they looked different. Can you see any horses and
jockeys that look the same in these two pictures?

New Orleans

Many of Degas's relatives ran a cotton business in New Orleans. Degas painted this picture when he visited. His uncle is sitting in the **foreground** checking the cotton. His brother René is reading the paper. His other brother, Achille, is leaning against a window on the wall.

The Impressionists

Degas was friends with a group of artists called "Impressionists." This painting was the first Impressionist work bought by a museum. An **art critic** called them Impressionists as an insult. The critic thought their paintings looked unfinished. Degas preferred to call himself a "realist" or an "independent."

A Cotton Office in New Orleans, 1873. This was Degas's only painting that was bought by a museum while he was alive!

Miss La La

Performers fascinated Degas. Night after night Degas went to the circus to watch Miss La La's unusual circus act. The famous circus performer would clench a rope between her teeth. She was then hauled up 70 feet (21.3 m) into the circus roof, held only by her gripping teeth!

Miss La La, sketch, 1879

Degas painted from his own sketches. He made many sketches and pastel drawings of the circus tent and Miss La La. In this sketch you can see where Degas changed his mind about the position of the arms and legs. The view from below makes the painting very dramatic and exciting.

Miss La La at the Cirque Fernando, 1879

Degas and the Dancers

Degas loved to paint ballet dancers. The ballet was very popular in Paris at the time, and the paintings sold well. Degas preferred to paint the dancers **rehearsing** rather than actually performing. He liked to show the hard work that went into putting on a performance.

Degas's pastel drawing *The Blue Dancers* shows the ballerinas backstage. Some are adjusting their costumes. Others are doing their warm-up exercises. A little like in his racehorse paintings, Degas liked to paint the tension before the ballerinas went onstage.

The Blue Dancers, 1899

The Dance Class

In this painting Degas shows tired dancers at the end of a long ballet rehearsal. The floorboards help lead your eye along the painting. Can you see the dog?

Unusual Views

Degas liked to paint from unusual viewpoints. He often **cropped** his paintings so that the people or things in them were half off the edge of the canvas! He did this on the racehorse paintings on pages 10 and 11, too.

Degas created this painting of a ballet performance from a very unusual **viewpoint**. The men in the foreground are the orchestra. The painting's viewpoint makes you feel you are at the performance, sitting behind the musicians as they play!

Musicians in the Orchestra, 1872

Place de la Concorde, 1875

Degas and Photography

Photography was just becoming popular in the late 1800s. Degas's paintings were influenced by this new technology. He took photographs and used them as **references** for his paintings. He liked the way a photograph captured a moment. His paintings often look as if they were photographs. In the painting *Place de la Concorde*, it looks a little as if the people are wandering through the painting by mistake!

Wide Angles

Degas liked to experiment with unusual shapes. He did a series of paintings of ballet scenes on very wide **canvases**. A similar technique was being used in photography at the time. Special cameras created wide shots called "panoramas."

In *The Dance Lesson*, the dancers are relaxing after class. *Before the Ballet* shows the dancers stretching and getting ready for their performance. There is so much to look at in these paintings. As your eye moves from left to right, and from foreground to background, it almost seems like the figures are moving!

Before the Ballet, around 1891

The Dance Lesson, 1879

Faces and Body Types

Degas was interested in different body types, and how a person's body type could affect the type of job they could do. His ballerinas were generally small, athletic, and slender. The laundry women he painted tended to be stronger and heavier. Degas's "realist" style meant he did not want to flatter his subjects, but paint them how they were.

In Degas's time some people believed that you could tell if someone was a criminal from their face shape! Degas was fascinated by this idea. He went to a trial of three young men accused of murder. He sketched the men's features. He described the pastel drawing on the right as showing the features of a criminal!

Degas's court sketch

Woman Ironing, 1887

In a Café

One of Degas's best known paintings is *In a Café*, also called *The Absinthe Drinker*. The green drink in the woman's glass is called absinthe. Art critics didn't like the painting. At one show, people booed the picture until it was taken down! Critics thought the two figures looked too down-and-out to make a nice painting.

Degas's friends modeled for the painting. Ellen André was an actress and artist's model. Marcellin Desboutin was an artist and engraver. People recognized them from the painting and thought they were bad people. Degas was forced to say in public that they were not down-and-outs, to save their good names!

Japanese Art

Degas's paintings were influenced by Japanese art. Japanese artists often put the main subject at one edge of a picture. They used strong shapes, like these rectangular tables, too. Do you notice anything strange about the tables? They don't have any legs!

Bad Eyesight

Degas began to suffer from failing eyesight in middle age. His paintings began to lose their detail. He started to work more in pastels as he could see the colors more easily. He also started to create sculpture. Sculpting allowed him to shape his figures, without needing to see well.

The Little Dancer

Degas made his models out of wax. His statue, *Little Dancer - Aged Fourteen*, has real hair and a real costume made of linen and muslin. The shoes are made of satin. The girl who posed for the sculpture was named Marie. She was training to be a ballerina at the ballet school.

Degas sculpted racehorses. He knew their shape so well from all the paintings that he had done before.

Degas's poor eyesight upset him. He could not paint outside because the daylight affected his eyes. He painted in a darkened studio and wore dark glasses. Some art experts believe that his failing eyesight changed Degas's style of painting. They believe that Degas did not change style on purpose. He could not see well enough to paint the same as he had before.

Degas's Last Years

In his last years Degas became almost totally blind. His artist friend, Mary Cassatt, contacted his niece, who then came to care for him. He enjoyed wandering in the streets of Paris during his last days with her and his housekeeper.

Some of Degas's last pastel drawings have become his most admired works! The famous painter Auguste Renoir believed that if Degas had died when his eyesight was perfect, his work would have been thought of as just "good" art. The work he did once his eyesight had failed was "great" art!

Dancers with Yellow Skirts, 1903. Degas did not often date or sign his later works.

Degas died in 1917 at 83. He was buried in the family grave in Paris. Artists Claude Monet and Mary Cassatt went to the funeral.

Degas family grave in a cemetery in Paris. Degas did not like the spelling "de Gas" and had changed his surname when he was young.

Degas's Legacy

Degas was a great artist and one of the founders of Impressionism. His work influenced other artists, in particular Mary Cassatt and Henri de Toulouse-Lautrec.

A self-portrait photograph by Degas when he was 61

Glossary

art critic
(ART KRIH-tik)
A person who judges
works of art as their job.

canvases
(KAN-vuh-sehz)
Pieces of cloth used as a
surface for painting.

cropped (KROPT)
Removed the outer
parts of an image such
as a photograph.

detail (DEE-tayl)
A small part or feature.

foreground
(FOR-grownd)
The part of a scene or
picture that is nearest
to the viewer.

masterpiece
(MAS-tur-pees)
A work done with
great skill, such as an
artistic achievement.

pastel (pa-STEL)
A crayon made by
grinding color into
a paste.

portraits (POR-trets)
Pictures of a person usually showing the face.

references (REH-fren-sez)
Things used as a source of information in order to do something.

rehearsing (ree-HER-sing)
Practicing for a public performance.

sketches (SKEH-chez)
Rough drawings representing the chief features of an object or scene.

studio (STOO-dee-oh)
The working place of an artist.

viewpoint (VYOO-poynt)
A position from which something is observed.

Websites

For web resources related to the subject of this book, go to:
www.windmillbooks.com/weblinks
and select this book's title.

Read More

Cocca-Leffler, Maryann. *Edgar Degas: Paintings That Dance* (Smart about the Arts). New York, NY: Grosset & Dunlap, 2001.

Mis, Melody S. *Edgar Degas* (Meet the Artist). New York: PowerKids Press, 2007.

Venezia, Mike. *Edgar Degas* (Getting to Know the World's Greatest Artists). New York, NY: Children's Press, 2001.

Index